A New Euphoric Gender: This Man & Wombed Man Emerging As 1… A Passionate Autocratic Kingdom Surpassing Time And Space.

Injustice's inception is the valley of envy (that never needed to exist), Which at its peak, unveiled and gave birth to the infancy of jealousy, which when it was nurtured grew to the maturity of a strategic plan of trickery to heist the Royal One's Rightful Place in the Cosmos and in Society Pre-Incarnation.

What I feel for you is anarchic melodic Rock. My Love for you is unstructured yet there are sensuous harmonic ravenous chords I'd like to pluck forever on your body that's structured like a curvy yet erect disciplined aroused love symbol guitar.This is how the PRINCE is Ravished over His MUSE.

The Wise One said to His MUSE "OH How I WORSHIP YOU MY NAUGHTY ONE, LET ME CLEAR THE OBSCURITY MY CARAMEL ONE. I WORSHIP YOUR BEAUTIFULLY SCULPTED ASS THAT WAS SCULPTED ESPECIALLY FOR ME BY OUR MAKER. I WORSHIP YOUR FULL SUPPLE BROWN BOUNCY BREASTS THAT BOUNCE UP AND DOWN AS I'M PENETRATING YOU AND YOU'RE MADLY THUMPING UP AND DOWN ON ME. I WORSHIP THE ETHER OF YOUR SUBCONSCIOUS THAT I INSTANTLY COMPREHEND ONCE I LABORIOUSLY PUSH MY THICK ROUND LONG ROD (THAT YOU USE FOR YOUR PLEASURE AND MY PUNISHMENT BECAUSE THE INSIDE OF YOU IS

TO MUCH FOR ME TO EXPERIENCE IT'S SO GOOD TOO GOOD THAT I THINK THAT THE WRATH OF GOD IS GOING TO COME DOWN ON ME AT ANY SECOND BECAUSE I HAVE STOLEN THE MIND, HEART, AND BODY OF HIS PURE INNOCENT ONE AND HAVE CORRUPTED HER, AND I NEED YOU TO CONSTANTLY REASSURE ME THAT IT'S OK THAT YOU WERE TRULY CRAFTED FOR ME) INSIDE YOUR NATURAL GARMENT.I WORSHIP THE SWEAT ON YOUR BROW THAT WETS MY LIPS WHEN I KISS YOUR FOREHEAD, THE SWEAT

THAT WAS SECRETED AFTER YOU HAVE FEVERISHLY
TAKEN ME ON A TRIP TO EVERY GALAXY IN CREATION
WITH THE WAY YOU HAVE JUST MADE LOVE TO ME WITH
YOUR BODY THAT'S REMINISCENT OF ALL OF THE ENERGY
FROM THE STARS IN EVERY GALAXY".

The Wise One Labored to Make His MUSE UNDERSTAND That she must Rule because He and The HOLY ONE Are Too Mesmerized and Too Much in a Stupor Over Her, the deference of her Character and of the lengths she'll go to and through to protect the HOLY ONE. HE SAID "YOUR THE ONLY ONE WHO CAN DO THIS, WE NEED YOU LOVE".

The WISE ONE'S WHOLE LIFE WAS ONE OF UNCHANGED
SUPERFLUOUS TRANSFORMATION.

THE LIFE OF CHRIST THE SUPERFLUOUS ONE, ALWAYS EXISTS IN THE VALLEY OF COMPASSIONATE SELF MARTYRDOM PRECISION OF EROTICA WHICH LEADS HIS MUSE TO EXTRAORDINARY PEAKS OF EXTREME FULFILLMENT AND EUPHORIC, ETHEREAL, ENIGMATIC, SOMETIMES ELUSIVE SATISFACTION.

Words Written are more solid than dress, dress is fleeting and is in constant change and comes in and out of style, but words and actions that are solid, and once transcribed are memorized, etched in minds and never goes out of style and last through the ions of time and is the solid foundation of which the New Age is established.

The Wise One thought whilst daydreaming about His MUSE: I adore you so, that once when we traded places, I FELL IN LUST, LOVE AND INFATUATION WITH THE LORE OF THE BEAUTY OF WHAT IT FELT TO BE THE WOMAN THAT IS YOU INSIDE AND OUT. WHILE I WAS IN YOUR BODY I LUSTED AFTER YOUR ALMOND EYES STARING BACK AT ME IN THE MIRROR.

I LUSTED AFTER THE CURVE IN YOUR THIGHS AND ALL
THE WONDERS OF WHAT IT WAS LIKE TO BE A WOMAN.
THINGS THAT I NEVER FELT AS A MAN AND I FELL IN
WONDERLUST OVER THE MAGICAL MYSTICISM IT IS TO
BE THE WOMAN THAT IS YOU, SO MUCH SO THAT WHEN I
REGAINED CONSCIOUSNESS IN MY BODY, I NEVER WAS
BEFORE BUT I BECAME ANDROGYNOUS NEVER WANTING TO

SEPARATE MYSELF FROM THE EXPERIENCE I HAD BEING
THE WONDER OF YOU THAT IS MY WOMBED-MAN!

When the Wise One awoke from his daydream he realized that he had hastily wandered into His MUSE'S quarters without notice and He had ravished her. Her guards didn't dare stand in his way. They did not want to succumb to the wrath of the Prince even if it meant that they were protecting the QUEEN, because they knew and understood that not even the wrath of the most Sovereign One compared to the Wise One's wrath if anyone stood in the way of Him and His MUSE. When the Queen encountered the Wise One she was aghast with astonishment wondering what is the reason for this gracious madness. She questioned why is my Prince pounding me so madly but she didn't dare interrupt Him as there were tears of grief, joy, and wonder coming from his eyes. She called to Him but He couldn't hear her as He was engrossed in His Daydream, He was overcome.

Finally He heard His Muse calling out to Him and He realized what he was doing and how many times he had climaxed a mysterious 13 times. He was not apologetic. He told Her let's do it now that I'm aware of what I'm doing He told her my dear when I'm done you will have climaxed 1,000 times and even then I will just have gotten started.

There are two Hells. The First ONE is to be endured, Which only a few will endure correctly and it is temporary. The second HELL is unendurable and Eternal and enduring it right or wrong is of no consequence as it will be a well earned heinous heartless torment with no reprieve or end in sight. Most of Humanity and their dark entities and dark celestial aides will have no choice but to ENDURE THE SECOND HELL.

The Wise One Understood about his MUSE that to everyone she seemed mysterious and elusive and a mystic puzzle. But For Him Personally He understood even deeper for himself why she was always unfulfilled and ever sad. HE understood that instead of being thought of as a distant wonder and as an unattainable peculiar mythical creature ions above everyone's

understanding and far above their reach, That
all she wanted, all she ever needed was for
someone, anyone or everyone to take just one look
at her and all of her manner, desire, intellect,
and intentions would become instantly legible,
and at once she would be understood to the one or
ones beholding her and that either one or all
would accept

her into their bosom and at once embrace her and finally actualize that her actions and intent is and was always for the good of and to benefit all in a humble delicate generous quiet kind and gentle manner and that she just wanted to be loved, and accepted, and understood by one or by all. But To Bad The Wise One thought "his muse He knew that she was so humble and her desire so simple and primitive that he knew in order for the wounded gaping hole in her soul to be healed and make her whole she would need the love,embrace,and acceptance of all(though she really believed that if all wouldn't except her she would be enthralled

and thrilled deliriously if she could get all of
this from just one soul), but Ultimately The
PRINCE Was disenchanted because He actually could
see into her soul even if His eyes were glued
shut.

And with this ability (He Possessed because He Loved Her Very Truly And So Deeply) She didn't Know, No-one knew, not Even God Who Made Him Knew that He Loved Her so deeply that every dimension of his reality even the reality HE knew as sleep was permeated with the transparent legibility of HER SPIRIT, HER SOUL HER ESSENCE, HER DESIRE, HER MANNER, HER INTENTIONS ever laid naked and bare before him.

And what he knew was that it was that way for all who knew her but for some reason it was blindly oblivious to her. She tried hard to figure out what she had done wrong to them or what it was that was bad about her, but she didn't understand that a malicious way of being and thinking was beyond the blueprint of her comprehension. But still all and all The PRINCE was DISENCHANTED because He knew that she needed the embrace of all in order for her to ever be whole. For HE KNEW but they did not know, For after all that's why she was made was to be adored and embraced by all and what ELSE THE PRINCE KNEW THAT THEY DID NOT KNOW WAS THAT IF THEY GAVE HER WHAT WAS NEEDED SHE WOULD MIRROR BACK TO THEM RESPECT LOVE ESTEEM EXALTATION ADORATION APPRECIATION GRATITUDE UNMATCHED AND UNMERITED BY THEM.

BUT STILL ALL AND ALL THE PRINCE WAS AND WILL REMAIN FOREVER DISENCHANTED BECAUSE OF THE HOLE THAT WILL REMAIN ETERNALLY IN HIS BRIDE, BECAUSE HE KNOWS THAT THE LOVE AND EMBRACE AND ACCEPTANCE HIS BRIDE IS AND WAS YEARNING FOR CAN'T OR COULDN'T COME FROM JUST ONE BECAUSE HE KNOWS THAT IF IT COULD SHE'D ALREADY BE WHOLE BECAUSE HE GIVES HER LOVE IN DROVES. AND HE EVEN GIVES HER THE RAREST OF AFFECTION THAT IS ONLY RESERVED FOR HER AND THAT DOES NOT EXIST FOR ANYONE ELSE NOR IS IT NOR HAS IT EVER BEEN EXPERIENCED BY ANYONE ELSE.

THE BRIDEGROOM UNDERSTANDS THAT LOVE AND ACCEPTANCE FOR HIS BRIDE MUST COME FROM ALL IN ORDER FOR HER TO BE MADE WHOLE, BUT AHHH AT LAST WE REACH THE LONG AWAITED DESTINATION...ETERNITY, THE WISE ONE'S UNCHARMED FEROCIOUS BITING VENGEANCE THAT CONSISTS OF OBLIVION FOR THE GUILTY OFFENDERS THAT LED THE KING'S BRIDE INTO A LONE APATHETIC UNFEELING BITTER COLD TUNDROUS DESERTED ABYSS THAT SHE WAS LEFT STRANDED IN.

THE KING'S BRIDE IS THE REASON FOR THE SUN AND THE MOON, BUT THIS FACT HAS ALWAYS BEEN ELUSIVE TO HER CONSCIOUSNESS BUT THE KING WILL SEE TO IT FOREVER THAT SHE KNOWS THIS FACT AND MORE!!! NOT JUST HER ONLY BUT ALSO THOSE WHO WILL BE SENT INTO OBLIVION! THEY WILL HAVE ALL THE MEMORIES GOOD AND BAD REGARDING THEIR QUEEN CONTINUOUSLY PLAYING THROUGHOUT ETERNITY LIKE MOVIES ENGRAINED IN AND ETCHED ON THEIR CONSCIOUSNESS BECAUSE ALTHOUGH THEIR SOULS WILL NOT EXIST ANYMORE THEIR CONSCIOUSNESS WILL ALWAYS EXIST AND WILL NOT ESCAPE. THE TORRENTIAL, TUNDROUS, VEHEMENT, TORMENTOUS WRATH OF THE KING! WELCOME TO MONIQUE'S DAWN THE LONG AWAITED UPPER ECHELON STATE OF BEING AND NO ONE LIVED TO SEE IT.

THE END.